HORSE FARM

THOROUGHBRED HORSES

ANNE ACCARDI

NORWOOD HOUSE PRESS

Cataloging-in-Publication Data

Names: Accardi, Anne.
Title: Thoroughbred horses / Anne Accardi.
Description: Buffalo, NY : Norwood House Press, 2027. | Series: Horse farm | Includes glossary and index.
Identifiers: ISBN 9781978580923 (pbk.) | ISBN 9781978580930 (library bound) | ISBN 9781978580947 (ebook)
Subjects: LCSH: Thoroughbred horse--Juvenile literature. | Race horses--Juvenile literature.
Classification: LCC SF293.T5 A33 2027 | DDC 636.132--dc23

Published in 2027 by
Norwood House Press
2544 Clinton Street
Buffalo, NY 14224

Designer: Rhea Magaro
Editor: Kim Thompson

Photo credits: Cover, p. 1 Olga_i/Shutterstock.com; p. 5 Vladimir Hodac/Shutterstock.com; p. 6 Wikipedia; p. 7 Nagel Photography/Shutterstock.com; p. 3 marinat197/Shutterstock.com; pp. 9, 19 acceptphoto/Shutterstock.com; p. 10 Sokolean/Shutterstock.com; p. 11 horsemen/Shutterstock.com; p. 12 OlegRi/Shutterstock.com; p. 13 Dennis W Donohue/Shutterstock.com; p. 14 Cheryl Ann Quigley/Shutterstock.com; p. 17 Anna50/Shutterstock.com; p. 18 Nina Dorozhinskaya/Shutterstock.com; p. 21 BearFotos/Shutterstock.com;

Printed in the United States of America

CPSIA compliance information: Batch #CSNHP27: For further information contact Norwood House Press at 1-800-237-9932.

TABLE OF CONTENTS

Meet the Thoroughbred Horse

Thoroughbreds, or T-Breds, are fast. They are some of the fastest animals on Earth! Horses of this **breed** win many races.

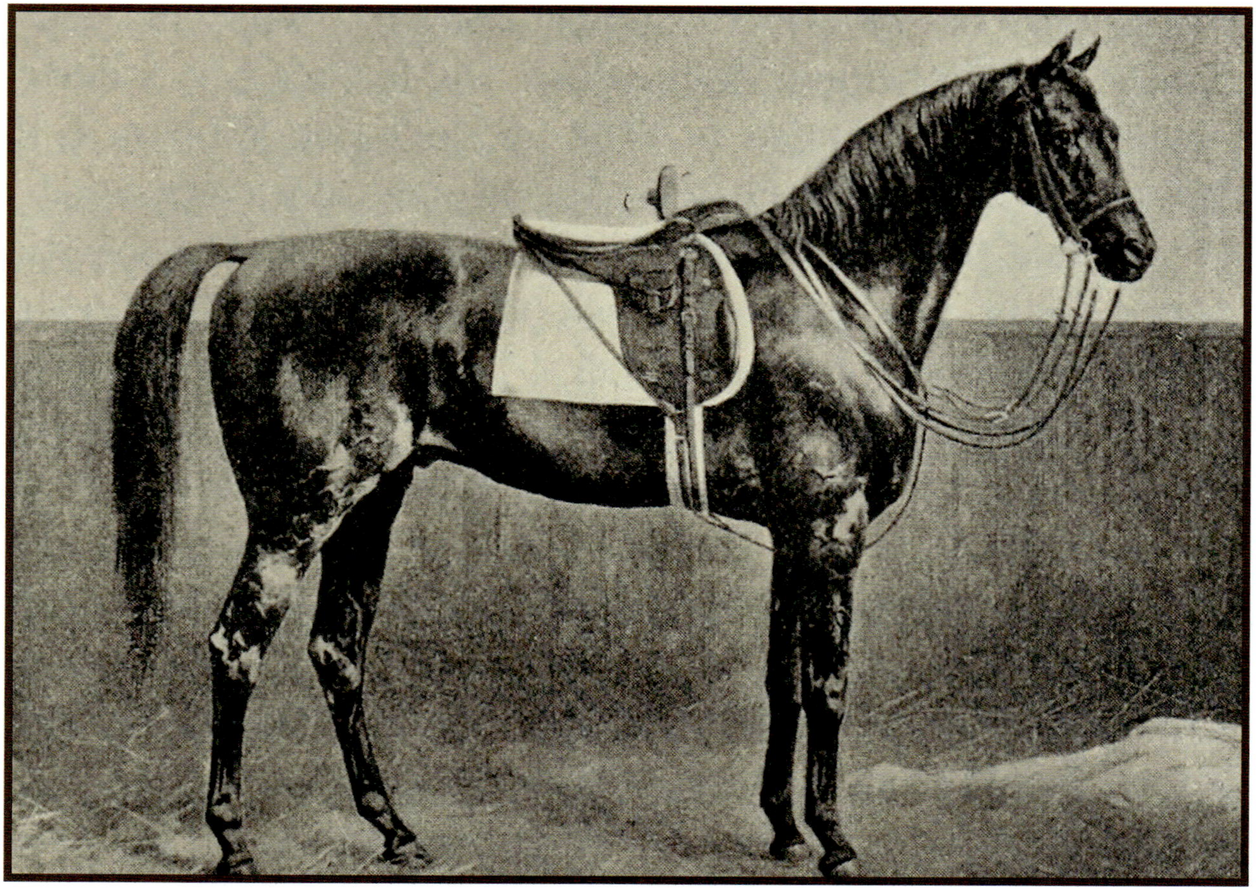

The first T-Breds came from England. For hundreds of years, people have bred these horses for speed.

Secretariat was a famous Thoroughbred. He ran nearly 40 miles (64 kilometers) per hour.

What Do Thoroughbreds Look Like?

A T-Bred has a **mane**, a tail, and four **hooves**.

The hair is mostly one color. It can be red, brown, black, or gray.

T-Breds have wide chests. Their bodies are lean.

Long, powerful legs help them **gallop**.

How Do Thoroughbreds Help People?

These animals are **spirited**. They are full of energy. They can be hard to handle.

Many **polo** players ride them.

G

Most racehorses are T-Breds. Some are good at **sprinting**. Others are good at running long distances.

T-Breds are not just fast. They are smart. They are hard workers.

People use them for fox hunting.

What Do Thoroughbreds Need?

T-Breds need lots of exercise. They should spend time in **pastures** each day.

They need healthy food. They eat grass, **hay**, and grains.

These horses have thin skin. They need gentle **grooming**. This keeps their coats clean and shiny.

Glossary

breed (breed): one type or kind of an animal

gallop (GAL-uhp): to run as fast as possible so that all four of a horse's feet lift off the ground at once

grooming (GROO-ming): combing, brushing, and cleaning

hay (hay): long grass that is cut, dried, and used as food for farm animals

hooves (hoovz): hard parts that cover the feet of horses, pigs, and other animals

mane (mayn): long, thick hair that grows on a horse's head and neck

pastures (PAS-churz): fields where animals can run free and graze on grass

polo (POH-loh): a game in which players on horseback use mallets to hit a ball

spirited (SPIR-i-tuhd): having courage and enthusiasm; bold

sprinting (SPRIN-ting): running at top speed for a short distance

Thinking Questions

1. Where do Thoroughbreds come from?
2. What are Thoroughbreds known for?
3. What colors can Thoroughbreds be?
4. Who rides Thoroughbreds?
5. Who was Secretariat?

Index

About the Author

Anne Accardi is a librarian who loves reading books and learning new things! She lives in Kansas City, Missouri. When she's not writing, Anne enjoys listening to music, exploring nature around the city, and spending time with her family.